1

Hiro Mashima

Translated and adapted by William Flanagan
Lettered by North Market Street Graphics

Ballantine Books · New York

A Del Rey Manga/Kodansha Trade Paperback Original

Fairy Tail volume 1 copyright © 2006 by Hiro Mashima
English translation copyright © 2008 by Hiro Mashima

Published in the United States by Del Rey Books, an imprint of The Random House Publishing Group, a division of Random House, Inc., New York.

DEL REY is a registered trademark and the Del Rey colophon is a trademark of Random House, Inc.

Publication rights arranged through Kodansha Ltd.

First published in Japan in 2006 by Kodansha Ltd., Tokyo

ISBN 978-0-345-50133-2

Printed in the United States of America

www.delreymanga.com

9 8 7 6 5 4 3 2 1

Translator/Adapter—William Flanagan
Lettering—North Market Street Graphics

Contents

Hello!
To first-time readers...
To longtime readers...
To those who just realized
they bought the wrong book...
To those who are saying,
"Who're you?"...
I hope you have fun reading this.
This is a classic story of the
friendship between humans
and cats.
Yes.
I got in a lie right from the start!

—Hiro Mashima

Honorifics Explained

Throughout the Del Rey Manga books, you will find Japanese honorifics left intact in the translations. For those not familiar with how the Japanese use honorifics and, more important, how they differ from honorifics in American English, we present this brief overview.

Politeness has always been a critical facet of Japanese culture. Ever since the feudal era, when Japan was a highly stratified society, use of honorifics—which can be defined as polite speech that indicates relationship or status—has played an essential role in the Japanese language. When addressing someone in Japanese, an honorific usually takes the form of a suffix attached to one's name (example: "Asuna-san"), is used as a title at the end of one's name, or appears in place of the name itself (example: "Negi-sensei," or simply "Sensei!").

Honorifics can be expressions of respect or endearment. In the context of manga and anime, honorifics give insight into the nature of the relationship between characters. Many English translations leave out these important honorifics and therefore distort the feel of the original Japanese. Because Japanese honorifics contain nuances that English honorifics lack, it is our policy at Del Rey not to translate them. Here, instead, is a guide to some of the honorifics you may encounter in Del Rey Manga.

-san: This is the most common honorific and is equivalent to Mr., Miss, Ms., or Mrs. It is the all-purpose honorific and can be used in any situation where politeness is required.

-sama: This is one level higher than "-san" and is used to confer great respect.

-dono: This comes from the word "tono," which means "lord." It is an even higher level than "-sama" and confers utmost respect.

-kun: This suffix is used at the end of boys' names to express familiarity or endearment. It is also sometimes used by men among friends, or when addressing someone younger or of a lower station.

-chan: This is used to express endearment, mostly toward girls. It is also used for little boys, pets, and even among lovers. It gives a sense of childish cuteness.

Bozu: This is an informal way to refer to a boy, similar to the English terms "kid" and "squirt."

Sempai/
Senpai: This title suggests that the addressee is one's senior in a group or organization. It is most often used in a school setting, where underclassmen refer to their upperclassmen as "sempai." It can also be used in the workplace, such as when a newer employee addresses an employee who has seniority in the company.

Kohai: This is the opposite of "sempai" and is used toward underclassmen in school or newcomers in the workplace. It connotes that the addressee is of a lower station.

Sensei: Literally meaning "one who has come before," this title is used for teachers, doctors, or masters of any profession or art.

-[blank]: This is usually forgotten in these lists, but it is perhaps the most significant difference between Japanese and English. The lack of honorific means that the speaker has permission to address the person in a very intimate way. Usually, only family, spouses, or very close friends have this kind of permission. Known as *yobisute*, it can be gratifying when someone who has earned the intimacy starts to call one by one's name without an honorific. But when that intimacy hasn't been earned, it can be very insulting.

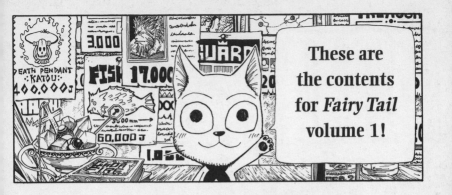

These are the contents for *Fairy Tail* volume 1!

Chapter 1: The Fairy's Tail

9

I...I need to take a quick break.

Let's go!!

If what we heard is true, then the fire dragon, Salamander, is in this town!

HAHH
HAHH

I can't stand it!!! I'm never getting on a train again!

FWFF

URP!

SAAAAVE MEEEEE!

KATAK
KATAK
KATOK

The train's leaving.

Ah!

KATOK

KATAK

Yup. Yup!

...your clothes will change color to match your mood!!

I already have it.

What's this?

TA-DAAH!

No matter what you're feeling that day...

Like this colors magic! Very popular with the lady wizards!

If you want powerful, that isn't it.

A white doggy!!!

Ah! ♡

Gates? Those are pretty rare.

What I'm looking for is a really powerful Gatekey!!

How much do you mean, really?

You wonderful man! ♡

BWOOM

Who cares! ♡ I've been looking for one!

20 Grand Jewels.

How much?

Like I said, 20,000 J.

No, I mean, how much?

12

Is my sex appeal worth only 1,000 J?!

KONK

TWITCH

Tsk!

He would only come down 1,000 J!

?

What's going on?

!

KYAA!
KYAA!
KYAA!
KYAA!
KYAA!

Salaman-
der?!!

TMP TMP TMP TMP

Salamander-
sama!! ♡

I can't
believe that
a famous
wizard-sama
has come to
our town!!

Y-You mean
someone who
can do fire
magic beyond
anything you can
find at a magic
shop?!

And
he's in
town?!

PAK

Maybe
he's really
good-
looking.

Look over
here!

Salamander-
sama!

KYAA!
KYAA!

KYAA!

Hm...
He's really
popular.

14

Say, Happy... you think this Salamander is Igneel?

Now I'm hungry.

You don't do well when it comes to moving vehicles.

I had to take two different trains!

We don't do well when it comes to money.

WOBBLE

WOBBLE

I'm even feeling a little better now!

Aye!

So we'll finally find him!

That's right, huh?

Yup. The only fire dragon I can think of is Igneel.

Aye!!!

See?! Speak of the devil and there the guy is!!

!

Salamander-sama!

KYAA!

KYAA!

KYAA!

16

KYAA!

He's so handsome!

I can't get where I'm going with all you lovely ladies here.

KYAA!

Ha ha! I don't know what to do.

KYAA!

W-Wait a minute.

I don't understand what's come over me!

B-BMP

B-BMP

B-BMP

Ahh!!!!

SQUEEZE

GLEAM

Or maybe I could be falling in...

WAFT

Hey, wait a second, brat!

Igneel!!

Igneel!!!

GRMP

Is that why my heart's beating so hard?!!

Is it because he's a famous wizard?

B-BMP

B-BMP

B-BMP

B-BMP

B-BMP

Ack!

SIGHH

It isn't as if he *meant* to insult me.

Now, now! I think that will be quite enough.

You'd better do some heavy apologizing!!

Right! Salamander-sama is a top wizard!!

Hey, you!! That was rude!!

Ah?

What's with you guys?

Ah?

ZIGGLE

ZIGGLE ZIGGLE

I want one!

Kyaa!

Here's my autograph. Now you can brag about it to your little friends.

SQUEEK

SQK

SQUEEK

Ahh!!

What a nice guy!!

SST

I don't want it.

I guess he wasn't the guy.

Gak!

SCREECH

Just crawl back into your hole!!

What is with you?!

SNAPP

Forgive me.

KYAA!

KYAA!

KYAA!

KYAA!

Ladies, my appreciation for your enthusiasm knows no bounds.

GWOOH

!!!

But I must see to business at the harbor.

VWOO

There will be a party tonight on my yacht.

Of course you all must attend.

KYAA!

KYAA!

KYAA!

KYAA!

What's that guy's damage?

He really is a piece of work, huh?

Of course, I'll be there!!

AHHHHH!

SHK

SPLATCH

GOBBLE GOBBLE GOBBLE

Okay, okay! Just take it easy on the food, okay?

You're getting it all over me.

You're ruining an expensive makeover!

So your names are Natsu and Happy?

Ah ha ha!

That guy Salamander is using a type of magic called a "charm."

This spell sways people's hearts in the magician's favor.

They outlawed the sale of that kind of magic years ago.

Anybody who'd use tricks like that to get girls can't be trusted.

CHOMP CHOMP

GULP GULP

GOBBLE GOBBLE

I may not look like one, but I'm more or less a wizard.

Myself.

Dat maigs zense.

GULP GULP

GOBBLE GOBBLE

But when you came barging in, you broke the charm on me.

MUNCH MUNCH

23

A guild is...

Oh!

It isn't like I'm in a guild or anything though.

MUNCH MUNCH

MUNCH

Ngeally?

STUFF STUFF

...a building where wizards gather and confer.

The guild acts as a mediator when it comes to wizards' jobs and information.

They say any wizard who isn't in a guild isn't a real wizard.

WIZARD GUILD

...are the hardest to get into!

But the most popular guilds...

There are guilds all over the world!

That's right!

Listen! Listen!

Mmfgl.

Ah! Sorry! You don't know anything about the world of wizardry, do you?

ub...

Oh, what'll I do? I want to get in, but I'm sure they'll be so strict.

It's a place where really incredible wizards gather!

There's one that I want to get into!

There are lots of big-paying jobs you can get there!

But I'll get into that guild no matter what!

By the way, you seemed to be looking for someone?

Aye. Igneel.

Y-You fink tho?

She's an amazing talker.

25

Hm? We're not looking for a man.

I was sure it would be Igneel.

We could see he wasn't a real Salamander just by looking.

...so we came, but it turned out to be somebody else.

We heard there was a Salamander in this town...

See he isn't a real Salamander just by looking? What do you mean? As a man, he wasn't...?

KA TAK

!!!!

Igneel is a real dragon.

And quit making faces like you never thought of that!!!

POIT

There's no way you'd find a dragon in a human town!!!

26

GWAA

TWITCH

Take your time and finish your lunch.

I have to go now.

SWIP

Kyaa!! Stop that!! You're embarrassing me!

CHATTER

CHATTER

CHATTER

Thank you!!!!

Thank you so much for the food!!!!

I got it!!

PAPP

Aye! We're in your debt.

But we didn't do it intending to save anyone.

I-It's okay. You did save me back there.

We'll call it even, okay?

I don't want it!!!!

SLAPP

You can have this!!

Salamander

What is it this time? They brought down the Devon Bandit Clan, but in the process destroyed seven private homes!

You mean Fairy Tail is creating problems again?

FLIP

SORCERER

Magazine:
Weekly Sorcerer
(Journal for Wizards)

Every party needs a celebrity.

That's only used for show.

Disgusting? Me?

Using charms! Do you really want people to worship you that much?

Not a chance! I'd never go to a party held by a disgusting man like you!

STOP

You... said you'd like to enter the Fairy Tail wizard guild, right?

Wait!

Who'd think a fool like you could ever be a famous wizard?

Yes, I have!!!

You've never heard of...

...Salamander of Fairy Tail?

32

Ah!!!!

ほぉ AHHHH...

Absolutely, sir!!

Then we shall meet again at the party!

I cast a pseudo-charm!!!

I'll have to stay in that idiot's good graces until I'm in, though.

HEH HEH HEH!

But I'm getting into Fairy Tail!!!

All right!!!

It's night.

Bwaah! I am so full!!

Aye.

POM POM

Aww! I wanted to go to the party, too!

Look! Look! That's Salamander-sama's yacht!!

Come to think of it, this Salamander was holding a party on a "yacht."

Maybe that's the boat.

Urk! I don't feel so good.

Stop getting sick just imagining yourself on the boat!!

Don't you know? He's that amazing wizard who just came to town!

Salamander?

34

!!!

You know! That famous wizard from Fairy Tail!!

POING

Urk!

Fairy Tail?

Fairy Tail...

SHUUSH

SHUSH

MURMUR

MURMUR

CHATTER

CHATTER

"Lucy," huh?

Such a nice name.

SMILE

SMILE

Thank you.

SMILE

36

First, we should pour the wine and make a toast.

GLUG GLUG

Don't you have other guests?

Never mind them.

SU-PLUP

SNAPP

The only one I feel like drinking with now is you.

Go with the flow. Go with the flow.

But I have to put up with it!

!

Now, that's just creepy!!!

Just open those beautiful lips...

...and allow these jewel drops of the fruit of the vine to dance upon your taste buds.

PLIP

PLIP

If you had just allowed yourself to get drugged, this wouldn't have hurt.

HEHN

What can one do with a girl like you?

GANCH

?!!

GANCH

Eh?

Who are you people?!!

SSSHT

SHUFFLE

SHUFFLE

SHUFFLE

SHUFFLE

Whoa! That's Salamander-san for you!

We got our first big-ticket item in a long time!

GWIP

What's going on here?!

Wha—

!!!

What is with this guy?!!

I never figured him to be *this* bad.

CHING

Gatekeys... So she's a celestial wizard?

Hm?

CHING

PLUNK

Only the parties to the contract can use this magic.

HUP

In other words, since it can't help me...

We don't know about magic!

Celestial? What's that?

It's nothing to worry about.

CHING CHING

46

Did I get her?

ZAPLOOSH

You damn cat!!!

I'm not trans-formed anymore.

Is that what Fairy Tail is all about?

Wait! First I have to figure out how to rescue those girls!!

GLUB
GLUB
GLUB

BLUB

There they are!!

I'm so glad they got caught in the shallows!!
♡

48

Now, Aquarius! Use your power...

...and force that ship to shore!!

I'm a celestial wizard! I use the keys to the Gates to the other world, and call the celestial spirits forth!!

SHUSH SHUUUSH

Did I just hear you say "Tsk" to me?!!

Well?!

Is that what you get angry at?

Shut up, little girl!!

Tsk!

GM

GM

GM

The next time you drop my key, I'll kill you!!

I-I'm sorry!!

I have one thing to say.

SLUUU

Wh- What is this?!

CHATTER
CHATTER

CHATTER
CHATTER
CHATTER

A ship just blew itself onto the harbor shore!!

WHOOOOO

Stopped...

What...

...just happened?!!

KRUMBLE
KRUMBLE

That rocking motion...

It's stopped.

54

DOO-GWOOOOGHH

KWOOOO

Can this even be called magic?!!

He eats fire... He punches with fire...

⋮
Oh, dear.

Of course, this enchantment was originally developed as a counter-weapon against dragons.

This is an enchantment that transforms one's body and gives it aspects of a dragon's body.

A dragon's lungs exhale fire. A dragon's scales dissolve fire. A dragon's claws are enveloped in fire.

What's that supposed to mean?!!

TWIK

He's a dragon slayer!!!

And Igneel taught Natsu all that he knows.

Wouldn't you say it's strange for a dragon to teach somebody how to slay dragons?

You know, I never thought to ask!!

GA-POP

WHAMM

Those idiots at Fairy Tail have done it to us again!!!

For pity's sake...

At least they reported that the damage occurred in the course of apprehending the criminal, Bora.

Don't jinx us. They may actually do it someday.

Someday we'll find out that they've wiped out an entire town!!!

This time, it's a harbor that's half-destroyed! Can you believe it?!

Why don't we just leave them be?

It's true that they're idiots, but it's also true that they have a lot of excellent people.

And that's exactly why they drive us crazy!

That's what makes this so awkward.

SIGH
はぁ

What did you say, you cretin?!!

I happen to like those idiots.

You shut your mouth!!!

Chapter 2:
The Master Appears!

Mira-chan!!

Yes, what is it this time?

MWAM

MWAM MWAM

MWAM

Hon-estly!

I want to be your next date!!

Hey, no fair! Wait your turn!!

Ah!

MWAM

Eyaa!! She changed into my wife!!!

POFF

You're already married, aren't you?

AH HA HA HA HA

89

Oh! Are you new?

POIT!

Isn't there a normal person in the whole place?

Wh- What's with this place?

!!!!

M-Mirajane!!!!

WHAM! BAMM! KRASH BOOM

Sh- Shouldn't you be stopping them?!!

Ah!

Kyaaa! It's you, in person!! ♡

It's more terrifying this way!!!!

GWIKK

It's more fun this way, don't you think?

DRRIP

Whoa

FLIP

Heh heh!

Kyaaah!!!

ZUKAMM

Uff!!

GA-WHOOM

Turn the other way!!!

Aaaahh!!! Where's my under-wear?!!!

By the way, you're a model, right? I can tell.

What's going on here?!!

SWIP

How unsightly! I cannot understand the indelicacy of these men!

Nobody lends out underwear!!!

Young lady, if it isn't too inconvenient, could you lend me your underwear?

GASH

I said, you're in the way!!

I will decide with my fists!!!

If you can't control your-selves...

A girl can't drink in peace in here!!

Aww, shut up all of ya!!!

HUSSSSH

Humph!

Tsk!

Oh,
yeah!

That was
a shock,
huh?

More
liquor!

HEHN

Master!

Oh,
so you
were here...

Master
?!!

Gray!

The Council? Isn't that the body that manages all the wizard guilds?

Huh?

First...

It's good that you rounded up that ring of smugglers...

...and in the end, you wound up stealing somebody's underwear right off the line and running away with it.

...but afterward, you stumbled around town in the nude...

But...I couldn't keep running around naked!

Maybe if you hadn't gotten naked in the first place?

SIGH
はぁー

Elfman!! While performing bodyguard service for a VIP, you attacked that selfsame VIP!

SHAKE SHAKE
ふる ふる

He made a crack about how "a man is only worth as much as his education," and before I knew it...

Loke...You seduced the granddaughter of the senior Council member, Rage.

Also, we've been sent an invoice for damages at a certain talent agency.

Cana Alberona, you drank fifteen full kegs of liquor at a certain tavern, falsely claimed it as "expenses," and worse, sent the bill directly to the Council!

So they found out?

In bringing down the Devon Bandit Clan, you destroyed seven private homes!!

You brought down the Tuly Village's historic clock tower!!

The town of Freesia's church is completely destroyed!!

You damaged a section of the Lupinus Castle!!

The observation station at the Nazuna Ravine is closed due to wanton destruction.

And you leveled half the harbor at Hargeon!!

SLUMP

And Natsu...

Me, too?

Warren... Krov... Alzack...

Bisca... Reedus... Levy...

etc....

So most of the stuff I read about in the magazine was Natsu's doing?!!

...have done nothing but make the Council angry at me!!

All of you...

SHK

But...

107

The Council can eat crap for all I care!!

GWOOGH

Listen!

GOBBLE

HUP

Eh?

Magic isn't some miracle.

Ours is a power that goes beyond the bounds of reason.

But it is born out of reason itself.

And take what is embodied in that union...

...with the wavelength of the world's natural chi.

What we do is match the chi that flows between us...

MUNCH
もしゃもしゃ
MUNCH

More than that, we pour our entire soul into it to make what we call magic.

...using our force of will and concentration.

If you spend time worrying about what those in authority think of you, your magic will never advance!

So don't let those idiots on the Council intimidate you!!

HEH
にひ

Thief Subdue. 160 Grand Jewels!!

"PLIP

Yeah. How about this one?

Let's do one with a big reward, huh?

Then it's decided.

!

No.

Isn't my daddy back yet?

But...he said he'd be back in three days...

...and now it's been a whole week.

Don't complain so much, Romeo. The son of a wizard should stay at home patiently waiting for his father's safe return.

I'm so worried!!!

Please go look for him!!!

It isn't that far away!!!

If I remember, Macao found some work at Hakobe Mountain...

......

Go home and drink some milk or something!!!

Don't even joke about that!!! Your father is a wizard, isn't he?!!

Any wizard who can't hack the easy stuff doesn't belong in the guild!!!

He may talk tough, but I'm sure the Master is worried himself.

He was pretty tough with the kid.

たっ,たっ,たっ,た,
TMP TMP TMP TMP

Uff!

You meanie!!!

WHAMM

Thief Subdue

160000

GANCH

Hey, Natsu!!
You broke the
board!!

REQUEST
BOARD

STMP

STMP

Master!!
I think
something's
wrong with
Natsu!

Eh?

STMP

STMP

STMP

116

But if he does...

...won't that just pulverize Macao's self-confidence?

CHIK

That brat never seems to grow up!!!

I think he's... going out to rescue Macao!!

Others can't decide your path for you!!

Just let what happens happen.

Wh-What's gotten into him?

Why'd he go off so suddenly?

SQUEE
SQUEE

I wonder if history is repeating itself?

Eh?

Because Natsu was just like Romeo.

You know, the dragon.

Natsu's father went away suddenly, and still hasn't come back.

When I say father...not his real father, but the one who raised him.

A dragon?!!

Natsu was raised by a dragon?!!

KA-LUNK

But one day, the dragon just disappeared.

I think that part of him is really cute!

Natsu is really looking forward to the day when he meets Igneel again.

So that's it...

That's Igneel.

Ah ha ha!

We Fairy Tail wizards...

!

We...

POFF

!

I don't believe it.

KA-KLOP
KA-KLOP
KA-KLOP

What we're wondering is, why are *you* here, Lucy?

What?! You've got some problem with that?!

HAHH HAHH

Actually, quite a few.

Aye.

And so...

Next time we both have free time, I'm going to hang out with Mirajane at her place!

KA-KLOP
KA-KLOP
KA-KLOP
KA-KLC

You know it's wrong to steal her panties, right?

Who'd do something like that?!!

GWAAH

Well, I finally made it to Fairy Tail, and I was hoping that I could be of some use!

You see?

And I figured that this would raise my stock with the place! I'm sure of it!!

Still, I never figured you to be so bad at traveling!

You can live with us at Natsu's place.

Once we finish our search for Macao-san, I'm going to have to find a place to live.

You poor, poor guy!

If I thought you were serious, I'd pull your whiskers out, Kitty-chan.

SNIFF

Huh?

F- Forgive me...

Are we there?

It's stopped!!!

GAMPH

Aye. She really is loud, you know.

Wait!!! How am I supposed to get home?!!

EYAAAH!!

Well, I'll be heading back to town now.

You're not wearing anything thicker!!!

It's cold because you're wearing thin clothing.

パキューン—!!!

BONG

BONG

Horologium!!!

Whoa!

It's a clock!!

No.

Loan me your scarf...

GWIP

KEEE

I-I-I c-command the G-G-Gate of the Time Keeper to o-open!

You said, "What'd she even come for?" and "What kind of work brought Macao-san to a place like this?"

...is her reply.

My Mistress says, "I'll be here if you want me."

What'd she even come for?!

Cool!

!!!!

You came without even knowing that?!!

He came to defeat the huge monsters they call Vulcans!

DOCHOOCH

WHOOSH

It's a
Vulcan!!!!

What Is a Guild?

It's a word you don't hear much nowadays, huh? They gave an explanation in the book already, but there may be somebody out there who still doesn't get it, so for that person, I'd like to go into a little more detail.

Originally, guilds began in Europe in the Middle Ages. You can think of them as groups of people working in a single type of industry who join forces and act on their decisions together. At the time, guilds were only for tradesmen and craftsmen, but for the purposes of this story, we thought, What the heck? Let's make a story about craftsmen whose craft is wizardry! And thus, this book.

So why did guilds arise in the first place? It's because the world is full of dangers. Tradesmen cross mountains and oceans to sell their wares. But there are pirates on the oceans and bandits in the mountains who are after the tradesmen's goods. Hiring soldiers costs a lot of money. So what to do? Well, why shouldn't everyone go together?!

And that's how many people with the same objective first gathered together. The danger never really went away, but they had more strength together than alone, right? One additional benefit was that the guild would take care of a tradesman's house when he was off on business. Eventually, the guilds became too powerful, and they were the causes of wars. But if you're really interested in that part, go do some studying. (Ha ha!)

In other words, a guild is where people with similar objectives congregate. In this story, the people are a group of wizards who earn their living by using magic to help solve other people's problems. "Earn your living" may sound a little too "grown-up" for some of you, but it means that wizards have a lot of adventures to look forward to. That's what the wizards guild is all about!

FAIRY TAIL

My name is Lucy!

I'm a seven-teen-year-old celestial wizard!

And because of that meeting, I became a member of a place where wizards gather, Fairy Tail, a wizards guild.

One day, in a certain town, I met a fire (?) wizard, Natsu, and a cat with wings (?), Happy.

It sounded interesting, so I thought it might be a good idea to tag along, but...

...he went to rescue the wizard from the blizzard-engulfed Hakobe Mountain.

But when Natsu found out that one of the Fairy Tail wizards hadn't come back from a job...

135

"What
have I...

...gotten into
here?!!!"

...is
what my
Mistress
says.

Uho
ho ho
ho!

Uh
Uho ho!
ho!

TWRL

TWRL

TWRL

TWRL

TWRL

And this
monkey is
way too
excited!!!

136

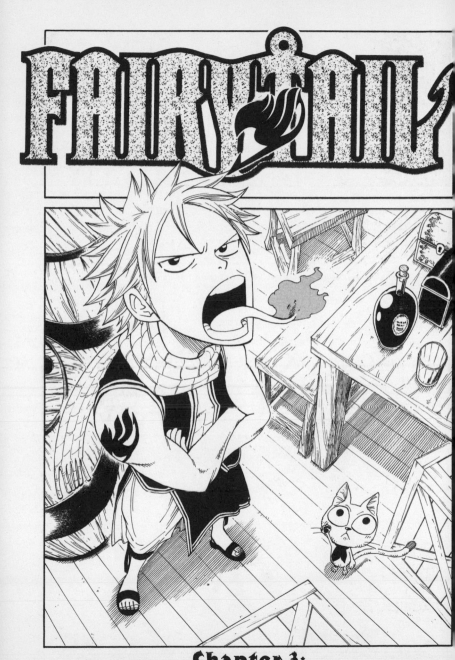

Chapter 3:
Fire Dragons and Monkeys and Cows

A girl! ♥

!!

I wonder if this is the monkey's lair?

But what's happened to Natsu?

POOF

!!!

STAAARE

W-Wait a second, Horologium!!! Don't disappear on me!!!

It's my time. Take care of yourself.

I want an extension!!! Please?!!

......

140

141

Your girl!?!

Uho! You no take my girl!!

TWIK

Oh, yeah. He's a pervert, too.

SIGH

Lucy-san!!! You are sporting a pair of beautiful udders today! Moo!! They're wonderful!

UNF UNF

No, I don't!!!

Don't say "My girl"!! She wants you to call her "My udders"!!

That's right, Taurus!! Go get him!!

Listen! Moo!! There's no excuse for rudeness!!

STMP STMP

And I'm a little uneasy spending my magic on Taurus, but...

I just used Horologium to his time limit.

GRIMP

144

Uho!!!

Moo!! I'm ready!!!!

The best thing is to make a blitz attack on the monkey and then go looking for Natsu.

Taurus!!!

TMP

That was good work pushing me out.

That...was... a...close... call...

Hm?

Natsu!!!

I'm so glad!!!

145

Ah!! Oh, yeah!!

PSSHUUU

Yeah...But didn't you want the monkey to tell us where Macao was?

That's decided it!!

But now it's been knocked cold.

MWAM MWAM MWAM MWAM

?!

MWAM MWAM MWAM

Wh- What?! What's that?!!

MWAM MWAM MWAM MWAM MWAM

Eh?!!

The monkey was Macao!!!

SLIP

"Taken over"?

It's a body-possession magic.

He was taken over by the Vulcan!!!

Aaaahhh!!!

SSLMM

Moo! Everything's all right!

GRABB

COW!!!

So you were a good guy after all!

Taurus!!!

Those are awful wounds!

It looks like he was in a pitched battle before he was taken over.

Macao! Hang in there!!!

Actually... I don't think he can be saved...

The medicine kit we brought won't be enough for it.

That wound in his abdomen is pretty deep.

HAHH HAHH

THROB THROB

So the Vulcan was a monster that survived by taking over human after human.

What do you think you're doing?!!

Gwaaaaahh!!!!

SHHHHHHHH

ジジュララララァ!!!!

Wai—

ボッ GWOOGH

I see. The burn is closing the wound! The blood flow is already slowing.

Lucy!!! Hold Macao down!!!

Aaaaaahhh!!!

Right now, it's the only thing I can do!!! Try to hold on, Macao!!!

Don't you dare die!!!

Macao, wait a little longer!!!

Dammit...

I'm ashamed of myself.

HAHH
HAHH

Hahh
Hahh

I... brought down... nineteen of 'em...

Ungaa!!

Ahh!!

Gaah!!

I get it! Now stop talking!!!

You're going to reopen your wound!!!

Unng...

But the twentieth... took me... over...

Gaah!!

Eh?

He went out on a job like that all alone?!!

You're kidding!! You mean it wasn't just one?!!

I said shut up!!!

You want me to punch you out?!!

It gets to me...

Dammit!!

I...can't face... Romeo like... this...

I'm out of my league here.

These guys really are amazing.

Wizards are just a bunch of drunks!!

And I wanted to be one when I grew up!!

All wizards are just chicken!!

They're only good for draining the town's liquor!!

Fairy Tail wizards are nothing!!!

Y- You're wrong!!

I... I'm sorry.

Daddy...

?

Daddy!!! You gotta go on some really amazing job!!!

As it is now... I just can't hold my head up in town!!!

162

Big Sister Lucy!! Thank you, too!!!

July 4th. Sunny, to blizzard, to sunny.

But it's fun, and the people are warm and kind.

Fairy Tail is really a mess of a guild.

...I already know that I'm going to love this place!!!

I'm just starting out as a wizard, but...

In the eastern end of the Kingdom of Fiore is the town of Magnolia.

Population 60,000. It's a trade town that's used magic since way back.

Magnolia

[Spain-like country] Kingdom of Fiore

...and you'll find the only wizard guild in the area, Fairy Tail.

Go past Kardia Cathedral, which towers above the center of town...

Fairy Tail

Kardia Cathedral

And!!

This is where I've taken up residence. (Rent: 70,000 J)

It's a little expensive, but the shopping district is close, so it's very convenient.

Chapter 4:
The Celestial Spirit of Canis Minor

I'm so glad I found a nice place!!

AHHHHH

A wood scent!

Pure white walls!

Plenty of storage space.

It's pretty big for seventy Grand Jewels.

And the most wonderful part of all is...

It even has a built-in kitchen stove!

A slightly retro furnace.

I'm the wounded party here!!!

Hey! Words like that can hurt.

This is a fine time to show your moral deficiencies!!

That's a crime!!!

What you two did is called breaking and entering!!!

Don't you know that there are certain rules of politeness even among friends?!!

づ" STMP
づ" STMP
づ" か"
STMP

!!!

Hm? What's this?

FLIPP

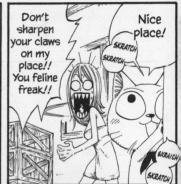

Don't sharpen your claws on my place!! You feline freak!!

Nice place!

SKRATCH
SKRATCH
SKRATCH
SKRATCH

FWAPP

N O O O O O !!!!!

169

I can't believe how selfish you are!!!

We came to have fun!!

No!

Who cares what it is?!!

Why don't you just go home?!!

Now you've got me worried. What is it?

There's nothing fun here! So drink your tea and go home!

I just moved in. I haven't even had time to get furniture.

Oh! I've got it!!

Just because I said drink and go home, I'm heartless?

Aye.

She just has no heart, huh?

How many celestial spirits do you have contacts with?

Six forms.

You count celestial spirits as forms. One form. Two forms, etc.

No way! It uses up a lot of my magic!!

Why don't you show us all of those key-guys that you have!

Besides, they're not key-guys! They're celestial spirits!

Horologium, the Time Piece constellation...

Crux, the Southern Cross constellation...

...and Lyra, the Harp constellation.

The silver keys are sold at magic shops.

There's the Golden Bull constellation, Taurus...

...the Water Bearer constellation, Aquarius...

...and the Great Crab constellation, Cancer.

These gold keys open the Gates called the Twelve Gates of the Zodiac. They're extremely rare keys.

But we don't have a contract yet.

Now that you mention it, I bought a key in Hargeon. Canis Minor constellation, Nikora.

Oh, man! They're going overboard on their reactions for no good reason.

Shellfish!!!

The Great Crab constellation?!! You mean shellfish?!!

SKRRT

A contract in your rear? That's gotta hurt.

What happens if a contract goes into arrears?!!

How did the conversation turn to my rear end?

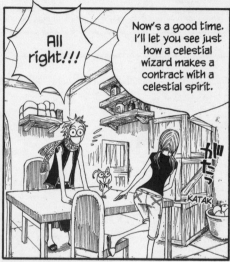

All right!!!

Now's a good time. I'll let you see just how a celestial wizard makes a contract with a celestial spirit.

KATAK

Just watch!!

Arrears don't happen.

Nikora?!!!

POP

Puuun!!!

......

STPP

This isn't a mistake!!!

PWIK
PWIK
PWIK
PWIK

I-I'm sure you can do better next time.

Natsu... I see an example of human egotism.

I don't have to use much magic to get through Nikora's Gate, and he's very popular as a celestial spirit pet!

Uh-huh!

A-Are you sure?

Puuun!

Ahh! You're so cute!! ♡

Can I call on you on Thursday, maybe?

Pupuun!!

Wednes-day?

Aye.

It's a bit simplistic, huh?

Pun!

Tues-day?

こくん NOD

Puh-uuun.

How's Mon-day?

ぶるSHAKE

ぶる SHAKE

Pu-puuun!

Okay. We'll go over the contract, okay?

さっ SHF

Shouldn't it be more complicated?

It may seem simple from the outside, but it's an important process.

Pupuuun!!!

There! The contract's all finished!!!

To a celestial wizard, the contract...in other words, the promise, is one of the most important things.

You can be sure that I will never, ever break a promise!!

!

ぴく PWIK
ぴく PWIK
ぴく PWIK

You mean it isn't Nikora?

That's just a general name for his type.

That's right!! So now I have to give him a name!

Really?

Plue?

Puuuun!!

Come here, Plue!!

たたたたっ
TMP
TMP
TMP
TMP

Puun!

It's odd.

Since Plue is Canis Minor, the small dog, I'd have expected him to bark.

Puuun!

I just think that the name feels cute!

Right, Plue?!!

Well, I don't hear you meowing, either.

ま ROUND る Puuun!

Umm...
:

SHUKA SHUKA SHUKA SHUKA

I... wonder what this is...?

TUP-TP TP TP

?!

Celestial spirits, huh?!!

You understood him?!!

GAMPH

Plue!!! I have to agree with everything you said!!!

PWIK
PWIK
PWIK
PWIK

But if you hadn't been there, things could have turned out a lot worse.

I never thought you'd come along on that trip, Lucy.

That's right! You really have to show more respect for the celestials.

It's true that I was saved by your cow on that snowy mountain.

Natsu, what is it?

Wh-What do you see?

I see...

If I really think about it, you're a weirdo, but you're trustworthy and a good person.

That could make me depressed.

The last thing I want is to be called a weirdo by him!!

!!

WHOOSH

Okay, it's decided!!! I agree with what Plue suggested!!!

Puuun!!!

Aye!!!

We have a contract, huh?

Yesss!!! It's decided!!!

Hey, that's a good idea!!!

Sounds like fun!!!

HEART KREUZ

TWRL

BAMM

And right off the bat, we have a job!!

Oh! ♡ You're so impatient!

See? It's all set!!!

They may make light of me, but they've accepted me as a valuable wizard, huh?

OH, HO HO HO...

....

200,000 J?!!!

If we get a book out of the mansion of this Duke Everlue, we get...

You're kidding!!!

See? A juicy job, huh?

In Shirotsume Town...
I may have heard of it...maybe not.

!

180

Duke Everlue

*Warning: He's a famous womanizer, lecher, and pervert. He is presently searching for a new blond maid!

Huh?

BRRRRR

Ohhhh, dear...!!!!

200000J

You planned this from the start...

True!

She can sneak into the mansion in a maid costume.

And Lucy is a blonde, huh?

And a celestial wizard always keeps her promises. How admirable.

This is awful!!!

GWAAH!

And I fell for it!!!!

Especially not for any cat!!!!

Just for practice, you understand. Just look at Happy and say, "Yes, Master!"

I'm not going as a maid!! You hear me?!!

Well, shall we be off, Lucy?

You tricked me!! That's so low!!!

FAIRYTAIL

Aww! I only hesitated for a few moments.

Yes. Natsu is off to invite Lucy along.

Huh? That ad for 200,000 J for doing Duke Everlue's mansion...

Somebody's taken it?

Ah! Master Makarov!

Levy, you may be happy that you're not going.

He wants to cancel?

No.

I just now received word from the sponsor.

That job may turn out to be more trouble than it's worth.

He's upped the reward to two million Jewels.

That's what he said.

CHATTER CHATTER

What's going on with that?!!

That's the kind of reward they give for military action!!

Tsk!! We just passed up a great-sounding job!!

CHATTER

Wh-Why would he do that all of a sudden?

CHATTER

Ten times the amount?!!

Two million just for one book?!!

...has just gotten very interesting.

It looks like this job...

KA-KLOP

KA-KLOP

I am the only master here!!!

I have maid my own hell...

How are you enjoying your ride in this horse-drawn carriage, Master?

HAHH

HAHH

Shut up, cat!!!

TO BE CONTINUED

Happy's Little Job

My name is Happy!

Fish is one of my favorite things!

REQUEST BOARD

One day, when I was looking at the request board at my guild...

...I found one of the most incredible jobs I'd ever seen!!

Let's Fishing

SHA~PING

I'd like you to catch an extremely rare delicacy, HanezaCana, the winged fish!

Your reward will be 30,000 J. Plus, we'll eat it together!

Besides, it sounds like it'll taste awful.

Oh, boy!!! Oh, boy!!!

You're acting scary.

Calm down, okay?

TWIK

Oh, boy!!!

Oh, boy!!!

Ohhh, boy!!!

Who said I was coming in the first place?!!

Oh, boy!!!

Then don't come.

?

What do you think you're saying?

But I'll get to see fish flying through the air, right? Who wouldn't want to see that?

It sure is.

She said that, and still she came along. I think that's cute.

I just have no interest in eating it.

186

They'll eat you if you don't watch out.

I wish you'd said that a little earlier!!

Right!! Now I fish!!!

I shouldn't have come!

You fish for Haneza-Cana here from this cliff.

I want to eat some HanezaCana!!!

I'm going to give this everything I've got!

Read a book, if you've got nothing better to do.

Go to it, Happy!!!

If you really want to eat HanezaCana, then hang in there. Don't give up.

Okay?

But none of the fish are biting.

I've decided to give up.

How weak-willed can you get?!!

Ehh?!! I thought I was cheering you on!!!

Lucy's picking on me!!!

So it was off to the house of the client for a taste-test party!

All right!!

SHAA

And when all was said and done, I had caught a huge load of fish.

SHAA SHAA

Try some fish!!!

ZWAKK

You think so?

This stuff's terrible!!!!

PTOO

CHOMPA CHOMPA

MUNCHA MUNCHA

CRUNCH

It's even terrible for you?!!

This stuff's terrible!!!!

PTOO

THE END

You really look like you're enjoying your fish. This has gotta be a happy time for you, huh?

MUNCH

MUNCH

189

Natsu's Design...

Huh? He had horns?

This is what the main character for the short-story version of *Fairy Tail* (actually, it's *Fairy Tale*) looks like. In the short-story version, he was a spirit, but this time he's human, and he's lost the horns.

( )

Nice to meet you! Or, long time no see! I'm the author, Mashima. First, let me say thank you for reading the first volume of *Fairy Tail*. Did you enjoy it? I'm planning on making things more and more interesting as we go along, so please join me for the ride.

In this portion of the book, I'm thinking that I'll use the space to talk a little about the behind-the-scenes parts of the manga, recent events in my life, weird things about my editor, or just silly stuff that means nothing. So read it when you have some free time.

For the first volume, I'll tell you the behind-the-scenes story of how *Fairy Tail* was born. Well, it really isn't all that "behind-the-scenes," but...At the very start, it was a story about a guild of couriers and how the fire-using main character, Natsu, carried various things on all kinds of assignments. Even though he's a courier, he gets motion sickness very easily. Natsu of *Fairy Tail* had his motion sickness as a part of his design from the start. The story of how he went from courier to wizard is like this: I pondered how to make the story about a man with a dream. I had the first story about the courier guild pretty much finished, but I became more and more intrigued. And when I came up with the wizard guild idea, and how all sorts of wizards could be gathered in one place, I had pretty much decided to change it to a story about wizards. I can't explain just how excited I was with the thought. One idea after another kept popping into my head. I practically forced my editor to allow me to do it, and I started over from scratch. That's how *Fairy Tail* was born. By the way, the title isn't supposed to be a once-upon-a-time story. It means the tail of a fairy. That may prove to be a pivotal point, but it may not. Well, who cares, really? [*laughs*]

So, from here on, I'm going to do my best to write an interesting story. We'll fly from one thing to the next. (What the hell is that supposed to mean?!!) So expect magic! Let's meet again in volume 2!

About the Creator

HIRO MASHIMA was born May 3, 1977, in the Nagano prefecture. His series *Rave Master* has made him one of the most popular manga artists in America. *Fairy Tail,* currently being serialized in *Weekly Shonen Magazine,* is his latest creation.

Translation Notes

Japanese is a tricky language for most Westerners, and translation is often more art than science. For your edification and reading pleasure, here are notes on some of the places where we could have gone in a different direction in our translation of the work, or where a Japanese cultural reference is used.

General Note:
Wizard

In the original Japanese version of *Fairy Tail*, you'll find panels in which the English word "wizard" is part of the original illustration. So this translation has taken that as its inspiration and translates the word *madōshi* as "wizard." But *madōshi*'s meaning is similar to certain Japanese words that have been borrowed by the English language, such as *judo* ("the soft way") and *kendo* ("the way of the sword"). *Madō* is "the way of magic," and *madōshi* are those who follow the way of magic. So although the word "wizard" is used in the original dialogue, a Japanese reader would be likely to think not of traditional Western wizards such as Merlin or Gandalf, but of martial artists.

Jewels and calculating money, page 12

In fantasy tales, no small part of the story's unique magical world is that world's imaginary currency. In America, fantasy writers tend to depend on their readers' familiarity with American money, attaching a phrase like "silver pieces" to an amount that would be wholly plausible in U.S. dollars. In Japan, the same convention is used, except that the imaginary currency is a substitute for yen. So, in *Fairy Tail*, merchants quote sums like 20,000 Jewels that sound ridiculously huge to American readers but are fairly reasonable to the Japanese. A rough-but-quick currency conversion is 100 yen to the dollar, so when Lucy is told that the White Doggy key is 20,000 J, that would be roughly equivalent to ¥20,000 in Japanese money, or about $200 U.S. Keeping the amounts so close to the yen/dollar amounts that readers already know makes it easy for them to understand how expensive things are in the fantasy world.

Kyaa, page 13

Kyaa is one of the most common sound effects in manga. It's a woman's scream, and it's a sound of either terror or delight. Yes, the same sound, *kyaa*, covers both of those emotions. You might think that this would be confusing, but actually, context usually makes it pretty easy to infer the author's intended meaning.

Master, page 32

"Master" is an English loan word that the Japanese have added to their language, but like many loan words, "master" has acquired an entirely different meaning than its English one. In Japan, the owner or manager of a bar or other similar establishment is called the master of the business. The nuances of the word "master" as we know it—that it implies advanced knowledge or skill—has disappeared in its Japanese usage, nor does it imply the "slave owner" definition. It is simply what one calls the person who runs a business.

Thanks for the meal, page 64

This is a rough translation of a ritualistic Japanese phrase. This phrase, *Gochisô-sama*, is said at the end of every meal. It literally means "It was a feast," and it is usually said to the person who cooked the meal or the one who provided it (for example, the person who pays the bill at a restaurant). So ingrained is this habit that one often says it to oneself even after finishing eating a self-prepared meal alone.

What's all this, then? page 77

Yes, this is an old, worn-out cliché that British police are famous for saying when arriving at a crime scene (although I doubt that all that many of them actually use it these days). But it is, in fact, a pretty accurate translation of what was said in Japanese.

Nekomander, page 112

This is a joking play on the name of the villain. The Japanese version used the English word "salamander" as the name of the villain. The Japanese word for cat is *neko*. As translator, I suppose I could have used the translation "catmander" or "kittymander" for Happy's dialogue, but the Japanese word that Happy used, *nekomander*, just had a nice ring to it.

Counted as "forms," page 171

Now, this was a pretty untranslatable word balloon. English sometimes uses special counter words for some items. For example, when saying how much paper one has, one counts by pieces or sheets. When saying how many cows one has, one counts by heads of cattle. This is a matter of custom and established usage. The same is true for Japanese, but on a much wider scale. Nearly everything has a special counter word. In the previous panel, Happy asks how many spirits Lucy has, but he asks using the same counter that is used for counting people. So Lucy corrects Happy by telling him they're counted with the counter *tai* (which uses the kanji that means "body"). Although, because they are spirits, "body" is not the most appropriate translation; the somewhat synonymous word "form" can indicate both corporeal bodies and noncorporeal manifestations. It isn't a perfect translation, since English doesn't allow for Happy to make his counter mistake without his dialogue sounding very awkward. But fortunately for the translator, it's in Lucy's character to explain a lot of things for no particular reason.

Nikor, page 172

The constellation Taurus is called Taurus, and the constellation Aquarius is called Aquarius, so why is Canis Minor called Nikora? I have to admit that I don't know. The

famous astronomer Nicolas Louis de Lacaille discovered and coined the names to many constellations, and the Japanese transliterate his first name as Nikora. But he did not name Canis Minor, and he seems to have no other relation to the constellation. If you readers know the answer, please write in to Del Rey and let us know.

Arrears, page 172

This was a pun. When translating a pun, one usually has to choose one of the two meanings to put into the translation (since it is rare that one word can contain the same two meanings in both languages). In this case, Happy asked if one must sign in blood (*ketsuban*), and Natsu misinterpreted the statement, saying that such a thing can hurt one's rear end (*ketsu*). As translator, I decided to take the low road by keeping the "rear end" meaning rather than the "blood contract" meaning. As it turns out, one does not have to sign in blood (nor does one ever come into arrears).

Maid my own hell, page 184

Another pun. In Japanese, one of the words for the underworld is *meido*, which also happens to be the way the Japanese say the English word "maid." I simply took advantage of the fact that "made" and "maid" are homophones in English to make a pun that is still a pretty close equivalent to the Japanese.

DRAGON EYE

BY KAIRI FUJIYAMA

HUMANITY'S SECRET WEAPON

Dracules—bloodthirsty, infectious monsters—have hunted human beings to the brink of extinction. Only the elite warriors of the VIUS Squad stand as humanity's last best hope.

Young Leila Mikami is one of the squad's most promising recruits, but she's not only training to battle the Dracules, she's determined to find the magical Dragon Eye, a weapon that will make her the most powerful warrior in the world.

Special extras in each volume! Read them all!

TOMARE!

止まれ

[STOP!]

You're going the wrong way!

Manga is a completely different type of reading experience.

To start at the *beginning*, go to the *end*!

That's right! Authentic manga is read the traditional Japanese way—from right to left, exactly the opposite of how American books are read. It's easy to follow: Just go to the other end of the book, and read each page—and each panel—from right side to left side, starting at the top right. Now you're experiencing manga as it was meant to be!